Herb's Tips for Living

Written by

Herb Pearce

Introduction

Many of you have enjoyed Herb's tips through my email newsletter for years. I enjoy writing them and do my best to live them! They are original, coming from my life experience and desire to write words of inspiration that support growth, love, satisfaction, courage and action.

Many of you have encouraged me to write a book about my tips and here it is! Thank you for that encouragement. I hope you can use these tips to live a more fulfilling life. Thanks for supporting this endeavor by purchasing a copy. Enjoy!

The tips are arranged in 23 topics. Each topic area is introduced, followed by bulleted tips. Take your time savoring and reading and rereading them. Many tips are repeated in different ways and on multiple levels to filter into your conscious and subconscious mind and heart.

These tips are written for you to consider. Certainly there are no right/wrong suggestions here, simply ideas that may make your life easier. Life can be complex and hopefully these tips will ease some of the stress that accompanies the complexities of living.

Herb's Contact Info

www.herbpearce.com

herb@herbpearce.com

781 648 3737

If you want to get my weekly email newsletter with Herb's tips and events, just send me an email requesting it.

Call or email for a personal phone coaching session or to inquire about my public workshops or team building trainings for organizations.

Herb Pearce is a therapist, personal coach and workshop leader in Arlington, MA, (near Boston) for over 30 years. He is well known for teaching the Enneagram Personality Types system as well as the Myers-Briggs and other workshops and trainings on understanding personality differences, enhancing relationship dynamics, and developing self esteem and spiritual consciousness.

Herb is the author of *The Complete Idiot's Guide to the Power of the Enneagram* and has taught the Enneagram Personality Types system to hundreds of organizations and to thousands of people who have attended his workshops. Herb is well known in the Boston and New England area and has taught in other parts of the US and Canada.

Photos by Herb Pearce

TABLE OF CONTENTS

Tips for Living

There are so many ways to learn and enjoy more from your experience of living. Life is a constant balancing act of options. Living requires action, compromise, and decisions. Enjoy your life process with its ups and downs. The following are some basic tips and guidelines to consider.

General life tips...

- Be grateful that you are alive

- Express gratitude more than complaint

- Allow all of life – pain, pleasure, joy, suffering, similarity, difference, up, down, direct, indirect, sideways – let it all be

- Allow this moment – free from past interpretation or future concerns

- Learn from the past, yet let go of it

- Focus on what you have more than what's missing

- Have a positive perspective without denying what is difficult or painful

- See goodness even when things are dark

- Compare yourself to changing states of weather – expect people to change as weather changes

- If you want good communication, offer good communication

- If you want respect, offer respect

- Be the person you want to see in others

- Have compassion for the humanness and insecurity of others and yourself

- Picture your goal, act, do the best you can and let go

- Have your ideals, yet live in reality

- Find what's in common - then talk about differences

- Work with the balance of seeming opposites

- See beyond your expectations

- Pay attention to what you want more than what you don't want

- See the world as a school for learning – be sure to take recess too

- Value differences in others as a way to develop qualities in yourself

- Everyone is on a unique journey that has rewards and challenges

Personal Growth

No one escapes the rigors of personal growth. Life doesn't support static reality. Evolution, challenge, and change happen. Growth requires some pain but less so if you aren't avoiding or holding on. Pain is lessened by acceptance, good support and guidance, and balance. Learn from those who have gone before and remember the courageous actions from your own past.

Newness and change can be both exciting and terrifying. The loss of the old may be a welcomed relief to the static nature of what is no longer working. Life pushes us, just as the seed in darkness waits for sunlight, rain, and air. Parts of ourselves are held in the dark until we are ready to experience ourselves in a new form, a new body, or a new thought reality.

Have faith in that which is unseen. Life wants to support what is good, whole, loving, creative and deeper. Listen to what is moving you, what wants you to be a different person - a person whose jump or leap will enter you into a richer, more expansive and connected you.

Tips for growth…

- Clarify where you want to go

- Listen to your intuitive instincts – follow them

- Get support and suggestions from people who have gone through something similar

- Growth does not require you to remain in a neglectful, abusive situation

- Your growth is not the same as another's

- Be cautious of people who tell you how to grow - it's often more about them than you

- What lessons are you learning?

- Growth can be fun and easy, too

- Prepare yourself in advance for the new you

- It's ok to grow slowly or fast – decide the variable speed at which to grow

- Do things in stages

- Don't bite off more than you can chew and digest

- Get feedback along the way before the next step

- Use toddlers as an example – fall down, get back up

- Listen while you learn

- Create stability while growing

- Hold onto what makes sense, and let go of what doesn't

- Sometimes we grow physically, other times emotionally, mentally, spiritually – each affects the other

- Things may be wobbly for a while until you adjust to the changed situation

- Enjoy the stability while it lasts

- Feel the excitement as much as the fear

- Take calculated risks

- Be thoughtful, not impulsive

- If impulsive, take responsibility for your choices

- Take responsibility for the results and learn

- A mark of a great person is someone who doesn't blame others

- It takes time to develop into the person you want to be

- Bumps and bruises show up

- The growth process can be as important as the result

- Be sensitive and respectful of others who don't want to grow as fast as you do

- Is it growth or recklessness?

- Don't compare your growth to others - unless you are evaluating a relationship's relevance to you

- The old saying – sometimes it's 2 steps forward, 1 back or 1 forward and 2 back – just hang in there

- Growth can be erratic

- Growth is more of a challenge in an atmosphere of addiction, blame, avoidance

- Sometimes the rewards take a while

- Growth rewards can happen more productively in the right environment – attract that environment to you

Mind and Thoughts

The mind creates thoughts, mostly from prior experience. It's easy to think our thoughts are real or that we need to act on them. It's helpful to evaluate and question the value or validity of our thoughts before action.

Often our thoughts happen to us without much control. Therefore, it's valuable to consciously create beneficial thoughts, as thoughts can be powerful. Being in charge of our thinking is very useful in creating the realities we wish for.

Thoughts can repeat themselves - rehearsing, worrying, and anxiously trying to fix a problem, instead of supporting us in positive ways. The mind is meant to solve problems, think, create, remember, plan, appreciate, etc. instead of worry, obsess, and torture us. The mind can create heaven or hell. Decide in which realm you want to live and be more in charge of your thoughts.

What are thoughts? Are they words or beliefs and statements we repeat to ourselves that we learned from our parents and other people? Our culture? Are they original? Are they biochemical? Why can't you control your thoughts more easily? Why are they repetitious and worrisome? How can you create and replay the thoughts you want?

Be creative with directing your thoughts and use them to your best advantage. Create and allow original thoughts. Let go of the hold of the past. Don't carry forward the pain of your past or the pain and trials of former generations you might have inherited. Let go of the grip that no longer serves you.

Primary thoughts happen first - then secondary reactive thoughts or judging feelings follow – "I shouldn't have.... I wish I had.... Why is my mind doing this...? What's wrong with me?" These judging thoughts and reactions are what;s most difficult and painful – not the original thoughts! Pain is the result of secondary reactive thinking and judgments.

Initiate, be creative, and be supportive in your thinking. Use your mind rather than having your mind use you. Replay less the scenes and feelings generated from thought and memory that no longer serve you.

The more you can witness your thoughts, the more at choice you are. Step back. Put energy, love, and direction into your thoughts. Let thoughts have the stamp of your own emotional power and creativity. Realize you are more than your thoughts.

Mind and thoughts tips....

- Notice your thoughts from a part of you that is independent from your thoughts

- See your thoughts as a part of you rather than the whole of you

- Don't believe every thought that runs through your mind

- Check out your thoughts against reality – see what is more actually true in regard to others or the environment

- It's fine to spend time not thinking – give your mind a break

- Let go of fighting with your thoughts

- Accept and allow your thoughts, then change them

- Notice the tendency to react to your thoughts, which just create more thoughts and inner conflicts

- Notice how thoughts tend to have their own world independent of you

- Think the thoughts you want to have

- Focus on thinking about what is good

- See fearful thoughts as a reaction to an imagined fearful future – bring your attention back to positive scenarios instead of worse case scenarios

- Be in your body and heart, as much as in your mind and thoughts

- Often our thoughts are more about how others and our culture have conditioned us

- Use your intuition which may be deeper than your thoughts

- Clean out your mind, similar to a lube job or oil change on your car

- Give equal weight to your thoughts, emotions, body, and spirit

- Use your thoughts instead of your thoughts using you

- Thoughts tend to create feelings

- Change your thoughts to create better feelings

- Thoughts and emotions are related to each other – they affect each other

- Your body reacts to thoughts, so have thoughts you want

- Think about present engagement more than past or future concerns

- Throughout the day, check your thoughts and give more attention to creating or paying attention to positive thoughts

- Your thoughts tend to create your reality

- Your mind is to be utilized when needed, not running 24 hours a day

- Meditate to quiet your mind

- Silence is powerful and rejuvenating

- Notice how fear and worry tend to create worse case thinking

- Remember positive memories, too

- Notice that the more you enjoy an activity, the mind is less obsessive

- Be kind to your mind – ease the criticism

- Observe the mind, rather than be the mind

- Question the truth of what your mind story tells you

- Practice positive thinking, positive memory

- Identify more with the observing mind than the revving mind

- Think the way you want - rather than how you've been conditioned

- Change your mental habits

- Let there be gaps of silence in your thinking - pauses, peace, ease, contentment, reflection

- Be willing to change the beliefs and interpretations you've had

- Be around people who have positive thinking

- Listen to positive tapes and read positive books

- Think about best case scenarios and what you want – let go of knowing exactly how you will get there

Emotions

Many of us are not encouraged to identify, experience, relate to, accept, or communicate our emotions. Emotional education is not in the forefront of education! Emotions take place in and around the body - a mix of thoughts that accompany body sensations and natural instinctual reactions to life experience.

Emotions are sometimes conditioned in us from our past, often from an unhealed place. They are also copied from or reactive to others' emotions, as well as experienced through genetic wiring, neurology, and predisposition.

We are very much a product of our past and others who have influenced us. At the same time, feelings are natural and original and an outgrowth of our own life experience.

I consider the three primary emotions sadness, anger, and joy, with fear being like a closure of emotion – another phrasing - sad, mad, glad, and bad!

Fear is actually a response to real or imagined danger and generally an anxious reaction to anticipated problems. Fear can include worry, doubt, negative outcome thinking, repressed excitement, concern, and anxious attempts to gain security. It's a response to bad things happening, tightening against unwelcome change, real or imagined, and requires mind management to release the stress created.

Joy has many aspects – enjoyment, humor, excitement, elation, positive anticipation, happy crying, or laughing. Sadness relates to loss or dashed hopes, but has many nuances such as grief, melancholy, nostalgia, regret, and empathy for others' pain and sadness. Anger can take the form of resentment, pouting, rage, repressed holding, irritation, or simmering upset. These feelings can be repressed or self-related or expressed to others.

Emotions are often encouraged or discouraged by others - which often translates as acceptance or repression of feelings. That which you cannot accept in yourself is not allowed in others. Family, group, and cultural systems often dictate the parameters of what feelings are acceptable or not, and it may take effort, challenge and acceptance of our individuality to counteract the "rules."

In Italian or Greek cultures, the expression of emotions is more acceptable. In England there is more suppression of emotions. Challenging the rules of emotion can bring up other emotions that have been suppressed.

Emotions can have an inner and outer expression. Inner emotions (felt alone) can be accepted or conflicted (a negative reaction to emotion or two or more emotions fighting against each other). You can feel or express emotions to yourself. You can write about them or yell or cry or talk to the feelings or simply relax into the feeling of the emotion.

Emotions are often countered with secondary reactions such as self-judgment, denial, repression, or a quick movement to another more acceptable, familiar, comfortable, or habitual emotion. Self-judgment can prevent the primary emotion from being allowed and even enjoyed. Some people express anger or sadness or joy as their primary emotion with the others held below the surface.

Emotions can change from moment to moment and be a challenge to follow, and like the artist's mix of palette colors, emotions can mix and match and become vibrant or muddied. It's normal to have more than one emotion at a time. Anger mixes with fear and sadness and joy. Someone might express anger with a lot of sadness and hurt beneath.

If you try to force or over-define your feeling without seeing and experiencing the full mix and experience of feeling, the mind reacts. Attunement to subtlety and the richness of inner life and feeling are essential to be with deeper layers of your truth.

The inner world of feelings is real, yet not necessarily reflective of the reality of others. Enjoy your emotional exploration and be open to learning, nuance, depth and surprises.

Emotional tips:

- Emotions come and go – at any moment be aware of their changing weather and atmosphere

- Allow all emotion to be felt – preference none – be familiar with all emotions – don't avoid anger, sadness, fear, or joy and their many manifestations

- Express from your emotion without under or over expressing – match up your inner feeling with a natural expression

- Emotions can erupt from desire and how desire is satisfied or thwarted

- Show your passion as it exists without excessive drama - drama can mask the real emotion

- Let go of ideas of who you should be emotionally

- Let go of rules about emotional feeling or expression that limit you

- Learn from others the possibilities of how to be or express emotion

- You can feel deeply yet have options to express how or what you feel

- Not expressing emotion doesn't necessarily mean there isn't emotion

- Cry when sad, show your anger without blame, reveal your vulnerability or real desire behind fear, and show the elation of joy

- Laugh, cry, dance, make noises - be your animal self - though be aware how others may respond!

- Let your body be a conduit to your feelings

- You have your voice, your sight, your smell, your tongue, and your touch – use what you have to experience and express

- Allow your feeling without mental definition

- Learn from your feeling self - be surprised by what you experience

- Open to that which is new in you - that which might scare you to see - that which expands your "definition" of you

- Let go of your past - be the newness that keeps showing up

- See the truth of what shows up in feeling and expression beyond your typical habits

- Listen to your emotions as they come and go - and then decide what to share or not

- Realize you are more than your emotions, yet respect and treasure emotions as they are experienced and alter

- Let go of ideas of what you "should" feel

- Notice the guilt that tends to show when you are feeling or expressing something new or different from your "program"

- Be aware of your feelings and let them be

- Watch out for judgments from others about your emotions – be your own advocate for whatever shows up in you

- Notice the tendency to hang onto an emotion – let go to what is more true in you now

- Feel as deeply into an emotion as is true

- Relax with feelings

- Let go of defining an emotion – put words to it as it needs words – yet allow feeling to be wordless if necessary

- Develop your emotional vocabulary

- Learn from the emotions of others

- Notice how you "copy" other's emotions

- Notice the layering of feelings as separate from the original feeling – first anger, then fear, then sadness, for example – feelings move

- Give yourself the full experience of each emotion as it is felt before moving onto another

- Notice judgment of feeling – more of a thought about a feeling

- Emotions can be your friend to clarify, nurture you, inform you

- Emotions can help verify your experience

- Emotions can instigate an inner dialogue to understand your experience

- You may be experiencing another's emotion as yours or as a mix with yours – sort it out if needed

- Feelings from your past can mix deeply with what's present – sort out what is true now

- Emotions give a more primitive and possibly truer explanation for what is happening

- Love your feelings – they help to explain your unique and ever changing self

Relationships

Life is about relationships. Everything is a relationship between yourself and something else. We are dependent on and in relationship to air, food, water, and many essentials that keep us alive. One cannot experience one's self except in relationship to another or life itself.

By nature, you are dependent on relationships for survival, feedback, mirroring and nurturing. Mom's womb, breast and nurturing, real and symbolic, are the essential survival mechanisms from which we grow, without which we would die. We are always in relationship with others.

Relationships are about engaging with the newness, the mystery, and differences of others – that's the opportunity - the learning, the process, how one can change in a positive way. The beauty of relating to other people, animals, plants, minerals, and myriad and endless life forms, adds so much to life. Curiosity, desire, need, and growth drive us to explore that which is beyond ourselves.

Relationships include pleasure and pain. Hopefully the pleasure outweighs the pain, but at times the pain outweighs the pleasure. Growth often requires pain, though less pain if one surrenders to the process and accepts changes that are necessary to grow.

Growth requires risk, and letting go of one's sense of stability to some degree. Relationships require adapting to different worlds while maintaining one's own. Finding and creating that mix is the process that helps you develop in relationship.

Stability and growth are two aspects that create and maintain a relationship. Stability needs growth for vibrancy and growth is supported by stability. Every relationship needs to find the balance between what stabilizes and the newness that comes from growth.

Change is natural. All of us are required to develop beyond the familiar, to aim for or allow experiences that expand and deepen us. Our daily world can be ever enriched by what we gain from relationships. One can learn on one's own, but much of our experience and satisfaction traces how others influence and affect us.

Relationships thrive on more than immediate behaviors. Consistent qualities of relating such as respect, caring, compassion, kindness, commitment and strength, are every bit as important as actions.

It's important to approach relationship with qualities that are enriching. What are the qualities that are important or natural for you? Which qualities do you offer? What is missing in you and maybe needs to be developed? What qualities do you want others to approach you with?

Respect is an essential quality to develop with which to approach your communication. Respect is felt. If you respect differences and communicate from that, whatever you do or say will have more value and will be respected.

We are often responded to with the same qualities we communicate with. Learn to respect different styles, gifts, needs, timing, defenses, strengths, and ways people love. No two people are exactly alike. Relationships require both adding and blending (wedding) and subtracting and letting go (weeding).

Relationship Tips…

- Accept differences as a natural part of life

- It takes real courage to go beyond the traditions of your past in your relationship building

- Any difference you see in another may reflect a part of yourself that may be hidden from you

- We are often attracted to difference in others to integrate that difference in ourselves

- Accept your need to grow and change

- Accept the pain and struggle that often accompany adaptation and change

- ·Look for what you have in common as much as what is different

- ·Bond with another in both your similarities and differences

- Be separate and close at the same time

- Learning to love yourself and learning to love another are related - one affects the other

- Accepting and relating well to your internal conflicts will greatly enhance your ability to relate to another

- Practice relating skills that enhance all relationships, not just your intimate ones

- View all relationships as sacred

- Let go of all assumptions about what relationships are supposed to look

- Have the courage to be your real self in relationships

- Have appropriate boundaries without walls

- Realize that hurt is often re-triggered from past hurts

- Lower or raise your expectations based on reality rather than fantasy, imagination or hope

- Be present with the experience you are having in this moment

- Be in your body and breath as much as your mind when you relate

- Care about another's world as much as you own

- Care about your world as much as another's

- Learn from another's world

- Let go of controlling another's reality – controlling your own world is task enough

- Be careful of the attempt to live through another – make sure you are living your own life

- Be independent as well as dependent – that is, interdependent

- Accept your need for another without fighting that fact

- Share yourself without overwhelming another

- Consider getting to know another before you enter sexual relating – which often distorts what is real

- Be both self and other-focused

- Time devoted to you and your self esteem adds to better relating to another

- Others don't want to do the self esteem work for you that you are avoiding

- The hurt from former relationships needs to be healed within

- Seeing and experiencing the dark side of life - the hurt, the risks, the pain, the misunderstanding - is part of the dance of relationship

- Have faith in the possibility of mutually satisfying relationships

- Managing the possibility of loss, rejection, and change requires courage, honesty and living in reality

- Value the learning as much as the outcome

- Be careful not to project your own reality or fantasies onto the other person

- Don't expect the other to give more than you are giving

- Taking another for granted can be a death knell for a relationship

- Let go of gender expectations

- Live in a state of appreciation, gratitude, and praise

- Realize all relationships change, even stable ones

- You are always in relationship to yourself as the foundation of relationship with another

- Know what you want in a relationship and how this relationship supports that or not

- Make sure you offer what the other really wants and not what you think they want or what you want

- Give to the level another can receive

- Relationships are *dynamic*, ever challenging your status quo and theirs

- See the power that you have in relationship to affect another – own that power and use it well for mutual benefit

- Connect to your vulnerability in relationship and accept the beauty of that

- See the vulnerability in others in their risk to relate to you

- Take responsibility for your choices

- Make a commitment not to blame others

- Relationships are a reflection of your spiritual growth – use spiritual evolution as your primary focus in relationships

Communication Skills

Relationships require communication, whether verbal or non verbal - communication about what you want or need, communication about what you are thinking and doing, communication about changing emotions, upsets, and joys. Communication requires clarity and some risk in order to be effective, the ability to adapt to others, the ability to assess yours another's maturity, and often requires caring, sensitivity, directness, and aliveness to work.

There are no definitions or rules to concretize the right way to communicate or what will work. Every relationship's chemistry is an unknown, a risk, and a puzzle to be unfolded and put together, yet the attempt to fit the pieces together is essential.

Pleasing others or being pleased is balanced against each other. Feeling close or drawn to another or not, affects one's communication and decisions on whether and how to share.

Sometimes it's best to share and sometimes not. Some people like direct communication and others like indirect and implication. There is no right way, no fitting a fantasy that everyone is alike or should be. Hopefully, the pieces land in a way that creates learning, satisfaction and good communication.

Communication requires feedback, adjustment, trial and error, attunement, nuance, play, dance, change, lightness, and seriousness. It requires being aware at any moment in time of one's self and another - letting go of the mind and its definitions and demands.

We all want to be understood in our world, yet the desire for our needs to be met can be overwhelming. A commitment to understand another in their world, fuels the desire for the same and increases the likelihood of mutual satisfaction. How does one focus on self and other at the same time?

How does getting to know yourself and self-communication increase the skill and communication with another? What can you do in relating to yourself that will have a direct positive impact in your relationship? What communication skills do I need to develop?

Tips on communication:

- Pause, more than fill the space with words

- Pay attention to another

- Talk less, listen more

- Spend time getting to know another before "commitment" conversation – unless you need to share your values

- Find the balance between talk and silence

- Communicate non verbally as much as verbally

- Understand another's nonverbal expressions

- Communicate your world to their world

- Share your story, not your monologue

- Downloading your brain is not communication

- Give as much information as someone wants

- Be as clear as you can be – it's hard for someone to fill in the gaps

- Be respectful in your approach

- Focus on desired best outcomes without necessarily knowing how you will get there

- Be clear and to the point with sensitivity and kindness

- Clarify what someone wants in communication – listening, solutions, support, suggestions, affection, questions to ask you, challenges to your ideas, etc.

- Clarify an ideal time to talk or amount of time to spend on something

- Check with another to see how the communication is going from their perspective

- Make sure you know the subject you are talking about! Let go of using the word "it". Clarify each time what the "it" is you are talking about to make it easy to follow.

- Make it easy for your communication recipient to understand what you are saying or thinking or believing or wanting - be as clear as you know how

- Appreciate and be grateful to the person you are relating to

- Focus on the positive possibilities more than the negative possibilities

- When someone presents a new idea, don't start off the conversation with "yes, but"

- Use the word "and" as a substitute for "but"

- Use "I" statements with someone who is afraid of the word "we" and "we" statements when someone is freaked out by the word "I"

- Never assume your worlds are alike – communicate from your world to theirs

- Check to see if your communication was received the way you sent it

- Thank someone for communicating to you, particularly if it was hard for them

- Find new and creative ways to communicate – use analogies or powerful images, act out stories, make sounds, look away from each other or at each other, walk and talk, draw pictures

- Communicate on the phone, in person, in writing, by email, texting, writing and leaving notes, voicemail, songs, through other people if necessary, hiring a mediator, counselor

- Take your time to respond though let someone know what or how you are thinking – which makes it easier not to project worse case scenarios

- Be reassuring or clarifying instead of leaving someone in limbo

- Talk about your different styles of communication

- Communicate judgments you have without blame

- Keep learning

- Let go of all assumptions about how communication is supposed to work – find unique and creative ways to be effective

- Learn from each other and attempt new and different ways and create habits of communication based on that learning

- Learn different ways people show love – acts of service, words of appreciation, touch, gifts, etc. – match their love language

- Communicate to yourself before you communicate to another

- Role play before you communicate to another

- "Center" or feel connected to yourself before and while you are communicating to another

- The intention and energy behind the communication is as important as the communication

Romance

What is romance? Who knows? Many societies focus more on practicality and appropriate matches by relatives rather than letting romantic feelings, desires, needs, fantasies, and longings determine partner choices. Certainly there's a question of how people choose each other, as people often choose poorly. We often choose those who remind us of our childhood caregivers, with whom we have unfinished business.

Romantic "choices" (it seems romance can choose for us) relates to cultural conditioning, hopes that another will fulfill our desires, projecting that another fits our checklist, idealizing another, and of course, sexual desire. Romance so often creates pain, as no one can fulfill fantasies that are unreal or imagined. Real relationships require practicality, reality awareness, being aware of limits, accepting what is important, and letting go of what isn't.

Songs galore talk about longing and loss, intensity and pain, unrequited love and illusion. Illusion will create pain, yet there can certainly be real romance, excitement and fulfillment that can be sustained, but only by seeing and accepting a person's wonderful parts beyond the fantasy. Seeing people for who they really are and loving that instead of longing for ideals (not so easy to distinguish) takes experience, maturity, discipline and humility.

Romance can lead a horse to water, yet the real relationship starts when the illusions of longing wear off. Hopefully real romance continues and the illusions are what wear off. Romance needs to be sustained by accepting human foibles, yours as well as others, appreciating what you like and how you benefit, new feeding of continued respect and appreciation, sharing experiences, giving support and gaining from each other's strengths, patience and love.

Have a romantic approach and relationship to life – spice it up, value what you have, initiate life to be special for yourself or others, make magic, value what's here and notice and create beauty everywhere. Imagine you are creating a newspaper with a focus on what's positive and real, more than problems, tragedies and the negative.

Think of romance beyond a lover/partner and relate romantically to your work, friends, hobbies and everything. Relating with excitement, depth and beauty repels lifelessness. At the same time, enjoy the simple beauty of flowers, clouds, daily life, the small things of life. The tips below apply to friends, special people and romantic partners.

Romance tips....

- Be in reality and still romantic

- Realize no one can fulfill everything on your checklist

- Go for the top 3 or 4 "must haves" on your checklist and let go of less important things

- Consider going more for good communication, caring, reliability, and compatibility more than intensity, excitement, and a constantly charged atmosphere

- Keep romance alive doing new activities, going to restaurants, going on trips, doing experiments, singing or doing art together, etc.

- Affirm and appreciate each other

- Leave notes, sing to each other, write poetry, be affectionate, tell each other the positive effects the other has on you

- Play word games, go to movies, read to each other, dance together, be interested in the other person's life

- Make sure it's mutual – where both of you are attempting to satisfy each other

- Enter each other's worlds

- Email a list of special moments you've shared with each other on the weekend or during the week

- Check in on the other's perspectives

- Renew your relationship – attempt to make it satisfying

- Listen with looking, handholding, sitting next to each other

- Remember special memories

- Focus on what's good and beautiful as much as loss, pain, what's missing or no longer here

- Have special memories for those who have moved on – alive or not – accept the coming and going of life – without obsessing on the past

- Learn from past "mistakes" in romance but don't dwell - have discipline to be alive now and forgiving

- Work hard to be in reality and ask yourself – am I putting the other on a pedestal? If so, why am I doing that? Will they be knocked off the pedestal at a later point? Do you love them or a fantasy of them?

- Be turned on by dew drops, rain, clouds, sun, rainbows, mountains, lakes, rivers, desert

- Be in love with nature, life, children, as well as a special other

- Treat yourself as a romantic partner

- Relate to a real person more than your idealization

SEXUALITY

Sex creates new life and is therefore powerful and sacred. It can also be fun, pleasurable and exciting. Sex can also be used to control, abuse, addict and cause harm. Like any process, it's multilayered, requiring awareness and consciousness to work well.

Some people love sex and the pursuit of the energy and reality of sexual relating. Some people are less sexual or even celibate to find a calmer, even-tempered way to relate to life rather than the more intense feelings generated by sexual or mate pursuit, and the desires and associated feelings related to sex.

Sex is a complex subject, fraught with excitement and dangers. Sex tends to create attachment and feelings of love. Pain can be experienced with the lack or loss of sexual, physical or emotional closeness or intensity. Survival feelings abound around sex.

Many people have been hurt with sexual or sexual/emotional abuse in various forms. Much may need to be healed and good choices need to be made. If others are not emotionally sensitive to you and your process, it might be best to limit physical connection with them.

Like all things in life – sexual engagement can be wonderful and/or anxiety provoking. Risk is involved and unknowns abound. Moderation for many people is a key – excitement and risk balanced with what feels secure, caring, somewhat predictable and comforting - different cycles at different times and different strokes for different folks.

For some people having sex with one's self is a partial or complete solution to the question of being sexual with another. Some people decide that it's too emotionally painful to have sex unless it's in a committed or mutually loving experience. Some people decide not to be sexual at all. Having sex, feeling close, dealing with sexual differences or being left can be just too much pain and trouble – why open the floodgates?

Often sex happens in the moment without much forethought – enticing, but risky. Thinking that you can handle sex and you won't be affected or attached can be an unrealistic strategy, though workable for some. Make sure you are living in reality rather than a fantasy or imagined or hoped for wishes. Make sure mutual agreements are real and not just to please.

Sex is an important area of life to relate to. There are many complexities - with desire for pleasure, experimentation, closeness, bonding, security, control and emotional and physical intimacy. Age, experience, intention, distribution of potential partners, varying needs of people and their histories affect choices and options. Add rationality to passion.

Sexuality tips…

- Sex is often a substitute for closeness, to relieve boredom, to gain excitement, to get some affection

- Find alternatives to sex through hobbies, work, passionate interests, friendships, love, affection

- Having sex with yourself in a creative, loving, and self-connecting way can be full in itself

- Accept your sex drive however high or low

- Make sure there is a give and take, two way street when it comes to sharing sexuality with another

- Much giving, receiving, active and receptive aspects exist in sex – expand beyond animal instinct driven sex only – though let's not put down animals!

- Keep healing yourself from any sexual abuse or hurt

- Be aware of how you use sex or sex appeal to attract or affect others – strive toward the right balance for you and others

- Be creative with your sexuality – don't get stuck in a rut

- Listen to feedback

- Realize people can be amazingly different in their sexual expression – what works for you is turnoff to another

- Sex can be tied to fun, freedom, commitment, lust, closeness, affection, intensity – many facets indeed

- Be aware of what "stage" a person might be in regarding their sexuality and sexual development

- Tune into whether your sexual stage of life or experience fits another's

- Communicate verbally about your sexual desire, attraction, feelings, differences, what you want – of course it's a risk to communicate but often a bigger risk not to

- Make sure there's enough overall real attraction to have sex and not just because you are "horny" or just to please – unless it's mutual and makes sense

- For some people sex doesn't have to be that connected to commitment, love, closeness and for others it's essential – make sure you are both on the same page

- Basing a relationship on sex and not on friendship or an emotional foundation can be too much like building a house on sand

- Sexual attraction does not mean you should be in a relationship with someone

- Sexual attraction is a mystery and often has much to do with moods, hormones, in-the-moment desires, image, seduction, closeness, intensity, depth, and passion

- Don't have sex if you don't want to – unless you see a self benefit or feel loving toward that person and happy to meet their needs

- Talking about sex is essential at times, particularly related to different needs and wants

- Some people like to talk during sex and some don't – you might need to talk about that!

- Don't get stuck in a rut – try new things

- Sexual inhibition often relates to or happens from moving too fast, not talking enough, not having the closeness or trust you require first, or from having different needs or perspectives or histories

- The more relaxed you are, the more sexual feelings may open up

- Sexual loyalty and agreements are important and often cause major rifts in a relationship if breeched

- Make sure you know what agreements or expectations you have with anyone you are relating to

- Listen to yourself and what you want, especially if what's happening is too limited, inhibited, intrusive or not rewarding

- Not everything is meant to last forever

- Associate sex with caring, communication, respect, and enjoyment

- If a sexual relationship changes or ends, make sure you have a communicative, caring, respectful, acknowledging process around it

Decision-making

Decisions have to be made and often there are conflicting priorities and consequences involved. Information may need to be gathered to help make a decision. The more one is self-connected, the easier it is to make clear decisions that support one's interests.

Choices can be overwhelming to many people. Fear of potential losses can freeze people in their tracks. What will I miss if I choose this? Why is someone pushing me to make a decision? Why are so many decisions and events pressuring me at the same time?

If decisions are made from fear of conflict or from concern about negative consequences from others, decisions are often put on hold. Being dependent on others' reactions can nullify what's important for you and keep you in limbo regarding decisions.

Feel what you will gain from a decision as much than what you will lose! Make a choice as an experiment, knowing that in many situations, you can change the decision while you learn. You don't need to know everything in advance.

Make decisions that best fit your needs as well as others. When you are pleasing you, you are more likely to be satisfied and likely to please others too. People want to see others happy, rather than miserable, indecisive, stuck and complaining. Being indecisive can be hell for all parties involved. Decisions can relieve tension and make actions happen. Tune in to the right decisions and right timing for you.

Decision making tips...

- Decide what is best for you

- Let go for now of what you might lose and bring your attention back to what you might gain

- Accept the reality of limited choices

- Say yes to parts you like and no to parts you don't

- Weight the options and possible outcomes

- Ask others who have made similar decisions what experiences they had in making their decision

- Be careful around listening to others who have a personal investment in your decision

- Think before you leap

- Some people make impulsive decisions to get rid of the anxiety

- Put attention on movement toward a decision, rather than worrying and avoiding the decision

- Get information, get support, compare to prior decisions and outcomes you've made before

- If someone is pressuring you, tell them to make their decision first

- Do be aware of the practical consequences of your decisions on yourself and others

- Be realistic rather than too idealistic

- Are you making a decision to be popular or to conform or avoid conflict, rather than what's really right for you?

- If you continue to remain anxious, maybe the decision you are about to make isn't right

- Do what is right for you even if others disagree

- Check out your potential decision with trusted others and get feedback

- Can you live with the possible consequences of your decision?

- Pretend you have made the decision and sit with it for a few days

- If you make a decision and realize it's not right, remake a new decision

- If someone is involved in the consequences of the decision, ask them how they may feel if you made a decision this way as opposed to that

- Brainstorm options, without judging yourself or others

- Include others in your decision making process

- If possible, don't make decisions under pressure or someone else's demand or manipulation

- If in doubt, don't make a quick decision or make it a "no" for now

- If a decision is right for you, it typically feels good afterwards

- "Bad" decisions often feel bad or create anxiety – (though if you are chronically anxious, even a good decision might be anxiety provoking)

- Make decisions under your time table – not to please others except by choice

- Connect to yourself, accept your feelings, be in charge of yourself – which helps with decision making

- Stay organized, to help make decisions

- Focus on the outcome you want

- Ask others who know you, how they think a decision will effect you

- Go with what you really want rather than what you think you want

- Be open to changing your mind at any point when new information comes in

- Let go of past decisions that might over influence your choices – be as present to the current situation as possible

- Clarify what the decision is about and what you may gain from it – security, enjoyment, pleasure, pleasing another, creating an alliance, supporting a relationship, excitement, adventure, relaxation, etc.

- Be as objective as possible, yet use your intuition

- Make a test decision and move ahead with it – see how you feel and how it initially works

- Watch out for impulsive decisions, too hopeful outcomes, naiveté, assumptions based on prior decisions

- It's ok to be ambivalent, confused, overwhelmed, etc. and still make the right decision, though those feelings may reflect concerns you need to identify

- Have some compassion and humor around decisionmaking

- Break the process down into smaller steps and decisions – it's less overwhelming

- Set a date to make the decision

- Talk it over with a few people without getting overly swayed by their opinion

- A final decision should feel right to you, not just other people

- Weigh the pros and cons on paper and place a percentage importance for each item

- Trust your gut and heart as much as your mind

- Be selfish! If a decision is right for you, it often will be best for others, too.

- If others hurt due to your decision, accept the consequences – you can't always prevent someone's hurt

- Clarify the values you are basing your decision on

- Calm down as much as possible in making a decision – have stress management skills available – such as breathing, meditation, visualization, relaxation, etc.

- Journal about your feelings around the decision

- Talk to others about your feelings around a decision as a way to feel ok and clarify what you need to do

- Realize you might be coming up against some painful memories around decision making that are "swamping" you with negative feelings – see if you can get in touch with those feelings first

- Accept your style of decision making – it doesn't have to be similar to others

- Learn from your decisions and don't repeat bad decisions

- Realize a decision can be made by default (by not deciding or letting another decide for you or for themselves) – accept responsibility for that "decision" on your part

- Don't be threatened by people who make quick decisions

- Don't judge or compare yourself to others regarding your decision making

- Keep relating to and calming your fears to be able to make more informed or intuitive decisions

- Trust decisions you make that feel right even if your mind goes into doubt afterwards

- There probably will be gains and losses with any decision

- When the decision is made, focus on the good that you gain from that decision with less attention on the real or imagined losses regarding other possible choices you could have made

- Ask others how they make decisions

- Get as much information as possible in order to make decisions

- Know yourself well enough to know how you typically respond to a decision that you are likely to make and consider possible options

Letting Go of Guilt

The United States as well some other countries tend to be repressed and therefore guilty - about sexuality, not working hard enough (even though it's a workaholic culture), being self centered (particularly if you are a woman), not making everyone happy, not being happy yourself, having anger, etc. It can relate even to having "bad" thoughts, not following tradition, being too individualistic, not conforming, not pleasing.

Guilt is a conditioned reaction to internal or external rules, principles and beliefs that you don't live up to or think you should. Most guilt relates to not living up to others' expectations and generally relates to past conditioning by family or society.

Guilt usually has its own self-punishment system, so it requires no outside intervention to reinforce itself – that is, we know how to punish ourselves. The punishment and uncomfortable feelings have been practiced often. The bad feelings often relate to past real punishment and shaming memories that you are now repeating.

There is also positive guilt, things you honestly wish you had done differently and feel bad about. Some guilt can serve a useful purpose to change unwanted behaviors that need correction.

Most guilt though is useless and actually damaging. There's a lot of programming in the culture (family, church, schools, media, etc.) to feel bad for thoughts, displeasing someone, not conforming, not joining something, in order to keep the status quo or pressure you into others' belief systems or actions. Make sure you are choosing your own values and decisions.

We are often programmed to feel bad if someone is unhappy with a decision we make or if we become too independent. Someone feeling hurt or upset, and blaming us for their discomfort, often induces guilt feelings. Our mind and body can go into automatic - feeling bad and stressed with guilt reactions (discomfort in the head and body and painful anxiety), when truthfully you might be doing what is right for you or even the other person.

Inducing or encouraging guilt in others is a way to control others, limit their behavior, and take the focus of attention off you. Some religions, corporations, governments, military and many authoritarian systems encourage guilt to control people. Guilt can be relieved by examining one's own belief system and "owning" what you really believe and choose to feel responsible for – by letting others have their own beliefs and by being responsible for your own truth.

Guilt is often specific to behaviors and specific beliefs; shame is more generalized to a broader context – just being alive and being your unique self, needing anything at all, etc. If you are shamed for normal experience – being human and having needs - then you are in double trouble. Just being an individual can be punished.

Making decisions for your own benefit - speaking your truth, saying no, doing something different than your friends or family, such as doing a profession or lifestyle that is right for you, can be life shifting. Being assertive, truthful, fighting for yourself, or doing what you want, can all trigger guilt reactions. Guilt can have physical consequences such as panic, breathing reactions, headaches, muscles aches and internal body pain.

Get feedback from people who support your truth, growth, and actions. Watch out for criticism and blame from those who want you to conform to their habits and perspectives. True friends support you to do what is right for you, even if it goes against their preferences, though possibly not their values.

Freeing Guilt tips…

- You are unique and have a right to develop your own beliefs and moral code

- Guilt feelings can reflect the displeasing of others, and not be a moral issue

- Reevaluate your values periodically

- Some people would rather blame another than see their part in the creation of the problem

- The more people take responsibility, the less guilt gets generated for others

- The more you do what is right for you, the less guilt you have

- Confronting issues directly can free up guilt and associated anger, repression and feeling stuck

- Don't assume you are guilty just because you feel guilty

- Get feedback from people whether you should feel guilty about a particular situation

- Live a fulfilling life generated by your own values and choices - allow some mistakes as part of the process

- Write a list of what you typically feel guilty for and be objective about whether you should feel that or not

- Forgive yourself frequently and allow yourself to be human

- Do better next time to feel more empowered

- Forgive others and help people relieve their guilt, particularly if it is based on others' values that they have adopted and not their own

- Ask others how they deal with guilt

- Make a list of your moral beliefs and do your best to live them

- Question what people say or do that may induce guilt in you

- Live with as integrity, honesty and commitment

- Trust your own innocence and good intentions and actions

Gratitude

Living with an attitude of gratitude is essential for a freer and more vibrant self. Focusing on what is good creates a positive feeling that attracts more of itself. Spiritual teachers emphasize that an attunement to gratitude in short time will create an enlightened state. If there's one method that attracts well-being, it's gratitude!

Gratitude fills you with abundance and like a magnet, keeps attracting what supports you. People like to give to someone who is grateful. It all depends on what you pay attention to. A grateful person often has a more fulfilling life because s/he pays attention to abundance more than loss.

The mind tends to focus often on what's negative. Train it to focus on what's good, positive, and hopeful. If things are 80 percent good but our mind focuses on the 20 percent, we are miserable. Attend to what is good and nurture that.

Appreciate your life. Express your appreciation more. Smiles and happiness will increase and everyone wins. Thank people you come in contact with and let them know the positive ways they affect you.

Start each day making a gratitude list of specific positive things happening in your life as well as a list of basic things that you often don't think about – the sun being out, the people who built your house years ago who you never met, the fact that you live on the earth, a rotating ball in the sky. Be grateful for the smallest thing. Share your gratitude with others, and be a role model of appreciation.

Some gratitude tips…

- Make a list of what and who you are grateful for, speak it out loud, think about it throughout the day

- Call a friend up to share with them what you are grateful for in your life today and tell him/her to do likewise back to you

- The energy surrounding gratitude is what's essential

- Be grateful for large or small gifts – the positive feeling of gratitude can as uplifting whether about small or big gifts

- Focus on what's obvious too – the sun is out, my contact lens work, my car runs, my computer works, I have a house over my head, I can eat, I can walk, I have air to breathe…

- Be grateful for and thank people who make the roads, build houses, transport food, checkout groceries, listen to you, people who help make phones work, forecast weather – the list is endless

- Be grateful for seeing, tasting, touching, smelling, hearing

- See the valuable learning you are having even in difficult challenges

- Make a gratitude list when you are feeling down

- Encourage others to be grateful

- Be grateful that people give you feedback

- Be grateful for the lessons you receive in life

- Be grateful that you aren't suffering as much as some people – for how lucky you are

- Be grateful for what you are learning when you solve problems

- Be grateful for material possessions, for friends, loved ones, groups, opportunities, work, helping others

- Be grateful for people helping you, giving you attention, sharing time with you, risking with you

- Be grateful for refreshing winds, birdsong, silence, rain

- Be grateful for parks, tourist sites, museums, restaurants, stores, services

- Be grateful every time you can pay a bill

- Be grateful for art, windows, TV, electronics, heat

- Remember what is good when things are difficult

- Be grateful for simply being alive

- Live in a state of gratitude all day long

- All day long think about what you like

- Be grateful even when things are difficult, but could have been worse

- Reset your mind back to being grateful, appreciative

- Express appreciation, thankfulness to others

- Let people know the positive ways they affect you, the difference they make

- Make a list of what you are grateful for every day – at least 5 items and aim for 20

- Let every day be a day of thanksgiving

- Smile even when alone just to feel good

Spirituality

What is spirituality? The belief that we are only our body and mind limits us. There's an inherent drive in many of us to extend beyond the boundaries of such a limited view of the physical only. Is our deeper self something more than what meets the eye? What keeps us striving for something beyond goals and successes and failures?

Is the inherent or deepest sense of ourselves non-physical? We are attached to our mind, thoughts, body, feelings, senses, desires and longings and think that is who we are. Is it possible that there's a deeper self, that is more present and loving, that notices all these other parts and maybe is the more real or deeper you?

Some people focus on religion or a set of moral guidelines or an established way to worship a traditional god or some form of sacred or ritualized values. Many of us have a yearning for something that also goes beyond the norms and interpretation by others, wanting something deeper or more individualized than what was provided in our childhood or traditional forms of worship.

Eastern religions, Buddhism, Hinduism, Jainism, etc., and other spiritual perspectives, such as Advaita Vedanta, tend to focus on the oneness of the universe. These spiritual systems focus on the fact that all the parts of the universe are connected and seemingly separate at the same time – the eternal mystery – the oneness among the many. Are we part of the whole or the whole itself? How does one relate to that which is infinite, yet ever changing? How does one include one's individual self, yet feel connected to everything?

Is your core essence spiritual? There are more questions than answers, as much mystery as scientific truth. The unanswered questions, and even the attempt to answer them are part of the unfolding spirit of who we are. Do we have a spiritual or etheric body that is different than a physical body? Trying to define that can be helpful, yet limiting if it's only based on what is already or traditionally known. Be open to new realities and experiences.

Many spiritual teachers have pointed to the observer self as being a key ingredient of spiritual knowledge. Love, loving detachment, presence, the mystery, neutrality, kindness, compassion, inner peace, and non-attachment are often associated with spiritual freedom, freedom from the ego and its endless expectations, pain and disappointment. How does one end the suffering of our wants and desires, which are sometimes met and then dashed?

Whether you pursue spiritual desire alone, with a small group or in a larger social context, much has been written about and experienced by people for thousands of years. Glean from this and listen to what draws you to pursue and know more. Listen to your inner voice, which guides you to a deeper truth.

Many of my tips below come from many years of experience listening to spiritual teachers from the tradition of Advaita Vedanta, a modern offshoot of mystical Hinduism, popularized somewhat by Eckhart Tolle. There is no right way for religion or spirituality. It's a constant process of discovery. Keep exploring what is right for you and resonates as truth for you.

Some spiritual tips…

- The deeper self is the one that watches and supports your life and is reaches beyond your individuality

- Your ego is transitory, changing all the time

- Your body, mind, emotions, desires, and needs change – your deepest self which is aware of those things - doesn't

- Awareness (God, Presence, Life) takes care of your body when you sleep – your heart beating, your organs working – are you the body or the One who keeps your body working?

- Your body breathes for you, grows skin for you, flows blood for you. Are you doing it? Who is doing it?

- You cannot define yourself completely because you are connected to everything – where is the end of you? Is it defined by your mind? Do you actually think you are your thoughts?

- There is no end to who you are – where's the boundary between you and not-you? Can you define it? Is your skin the boundary, the energy beyond the skin? Where does it end? What final molecule defines you?

- You cannot live on your own – the you who you think you are is dependent on everything else – food, air, connection, land

- Let go of the fight to be an individual – you have an individual ego but you aren't just an individual ego, except in your head!

- Individuality is a seeming aspect of reality, yet it can't be defined as totally separate – you are part of the whole whether you like it or not

- Be an individual in your mind but don't believe that's the deepest you

- Defining yourself will keep changing because the ego is always changing

- You are so much more than your relationships, money, work, your appearance, your body, your thoughts and your possessions

- Define yourself less from your accomplishments and more from what helps you do the accomplishments

- Notice the thought of the individual you - let it go and you will be happier – just enjoy life – let life live you

- Suffering is caused by the attachment to the "I" identity – you are so much more than this "I"

- Be the limitless self that you are

- It's all perspective – your individual pain seen from the sky seems less painful – from within the ego identity self it's very painful

- Enjoy your individuality without being defined by it

- Develop compassion for others, for yourself

- Be open to other worlds and other dimensions while staying grounded in present reality

- Look within, without and all around – life includes all

- Feel your eternal nature as who you are

- Ask others how they experience their spirituality

- Explore what is right for you – attend various churches or spiritual groups or traditions or experience other perspectives to see what is true for you

- Practice meditation, yoga or nature worship as aspects of your spirituality

- The noticing of your breath – a bridge between body and spirit - will be healing and relaxing

- Focus on an object such as a candle flame or a beautiful object to relax and softly focus

- Witness (stand back from your personal process) and be aware – pay attention to the witnessing as who you are

- Relax into this moment – allow it to be as it is

- Be grateful for what is – express gratitude (thinking about, writing, journaling, saying out loud, saying to friends) throughout the day

- Enjoy your unique self and also experience the connection to everything, the relatedness of everything

- See that all things are sacred

- Be willing to be wrong – admit "mistakes" – open to humility

- Be unknowing, innocent, guileless

- Allow the unknown to be ok – open to what may unfold from the unknown

- See that life transitions to other realities

- There is no total death, only of a temporary physical form – as all things change in life, as insects shed skin, birds molt feathers, leaves fall – everything changes form

- Everything changes and dies; all things lose and change their physical form

- Learn the spiritual lessons rather than be attached to an exact outcome

- Let go of some of your past history and conditioning – you are so much more than your conditioning

- Feel your essential self – pure, loving, and open

- Inherent traits of love and connection are inborn and often conditioned out of us – live your natural, inborn traits, God-given self

Fun and Play

Why grow up to be adult when it's so associated with lack of fun and play? When you notice the inherent joy of discovery of children, who's to say that should ever end? That excitement, innocence, exploring one's natural self - is essential. Life is meant to be fun, an endless discovery of the new, the different and what awe-inspiring.

Babies and kids see exploration and play as natural. Everything is a new experience, a new discovery, wonder and experimentation. Kids are less concerned with beliefs than experiences that are pleasurable and explorative. New sights, sounds, ways to touch and taste and smell are natural to explore and are the end result in itself.

With kids, repetition of what's enjoyable as well as the new, is good. With children there is less concern about appearances — ways in which adults protect themselves from being fully alive. Though kids have elements of control, power, competition, me, mine, etc. just like adults, there is an innocence that generally is filled with a simple honesty that's pure.

Of course everyone is different — some people are more me oriented and some other oriented, child or adult. Whatever the truth, the more you can be your real self and also have a fun and playful attitude about life - the more you'll enjoy life, as well as others around you. Have fun so others can enjoy being around you! If you are too serious, critical or withdrawn, you and others don't get to experience and enjoy you fully.

My friend Rick and Herb

Fun and Play tips…

- Have fun – enjoyable in itself – as well as helping others have a good time too

- Be your kid spirit – not letting responsibilities and appearances keep you from play, fun, spontaneity and creativity

- Explore what is new and different – always be curious

- Laugh as much as you want

- Explore games and experiences and people and adventures

- Let go of age as a barrier

- Play with and be around kids

- Learn while exploring new things

- Have creative pursuits such as singing, dance, drawing, painting, sculpting, gardening, etc.

- Have fun with everything – working, relating, working on your yard, washing dishes, watching TV, walking – try new ways of doing these activities

- Feel joy and pleasure in your body

- Watch out for habits and settled ways – they can disturb the fun of discovery

- Some disturbances in life are good to shake up cobwebs, old ways and that which is out of date – enjoy the process

- Synthesize old worlds into new realities – often the new, when adjusted to, is preferred

- Smile when alone – smile with others

- Live in the unknown and enjoy the exploration

- Let go of over defining things

- Throw away some of the rules, though keep the guidelines

- Be silly, play, and use your body in fun creative ways

- Try new ways of stretching, walking, moving

- Tell jokes, do stand up comedy or go to a comedy club

- Help others play

- Express your excitement and joy

- Laugh out loud

- Have fun with real kids and adult kids

- Go to a water park, amusement park, nature park, and flower garden

- Go camping, canoeing, hiking, swimming, do sports – enjoy physical activity and gain experience and skills

- Learn to identify plants, trees, birds and insects

- Keep the original excitement inherent in the human experience

- Play board games, word or card games (many local communities have board or word or card game groups)

- Make faces, wear new or funny clothes, Hawaiian shirts, summer travel clothes, hats

- Have a bunch of props available to act out scenes from life

- Try out for and act in plays or attend local community theater

- Write poetry, have a sketchbook, doodle, paint

- Be more outrageous

- Act out different parts of yourself, play charades

Relaxation

We are often stressed, overworked, too focused on concerns about the future, too caught up in the details of life and what might happen, too worried about ourselves and loved ones. It's easy to focus on problems - which makes it hard to relax and allow.

The more relaxed you are, the healthier you will be and the more aware and present you are, the more you will be more available for current reality and enjoyment. The key to life is to relax with what is, to use your body as a vehicle for comfort and letting go and openness.

Even when worried, remember what is good too. Memory for the positive will balance out the worry, which is thought absorbing and time consuming! Remember that worry is only one part of a whole. Much of worry and stress is useless, not focused on something that is actually happening but may happen.

The more relaxed you are, the less likely that something bad will happen. Bad things may happen more when we are distracted, distressed or out of touch with ourselves. Of course bad things happen to good people and no matter what you do, things happen.

Relaxation may require some focused letting go if you are used to stress. Notice the stress reactions in your body (in controlled breathing, thinking, tightening, pain) and release in ways mentioned below. Until you notice, you may forget to relax. Practice relaxing and allowing and it becomes more natural. Habits take attention to change.

Herb's relaxing tips…

- Notice and follow your breath (rise and fall of belly, breathing in and out in nose) and find ways to breathe that feel good

- Breathe more slowly with longer breaths and feel good

- Notice tension in your muscles and "soften" – relax some of the tension – allow gravity to take over - drop your shoulders for instance

- Scan the body and neck and face for tension – notice how subtle tension can be and "untighten" and loosen

- Visualize or post pictures of pleasant scenes or memories

- Surround yourself with pleasant and enjoyable sounds

- Have hobbies and interests that satisfy you

- Slow down in general

- Meditate, close your eyes, go in, and let the world go for a while

- Play relaxing CDs, background music throughout the day

- Set a time limit to worry!

- Create your lifestyle to be more relaxing

- Take a break every hour or two

- Have goals but don't let them consume you

- Live a more relaxed life now, not in the future

- Relaxation can help you accomplish more

- Fewer mistakes occur when you are relaxed

- Take time off for yourself

- Take time to recoup

- Do things to renew – get a massage, take a reflective walk, eat healthy foods, meditate

- Be around people that relax you

- Don't take on more challenges than you can handle

- Let go of the tension of competition and comparisons

- Only compete or compare yourself to yourself instead of others – and even then do it gingerly

- Notice when you are too serious and lighten up

- Say the word "relax" to yourself

- Exercise each day to give your body attention, stretching, and enjoyment – yoga, stretching, walking, aerobics, weight training, running

- Surround yourself with words, objects and experiences that relax you

- Focus on relaxation as much as accomplishment

- Approach action and goals with alert relaxation

- Slow down, you move too fast

- Imitate people who are relaxed – ask them how they relax

- Pretend you are a cat or dog stretching and relaxing

- Take naps when you are tired

- Approach life in a more gentle, easy way

Creativity, Hobbies and Interests

It's important to be creative – making something happen that never existed before, finding new ways of doing things and approaching life and experience with vitality, feeling and new twists. Whether it's drawing, canoeing, painting, dancing, teaching, singing, or sculpting, the mind/heart/body/spirit loves to create, to integrate or synthesize disparate elements and skills – to develop something new, often with depth, with fun, expertise, naturally developing skill and satisfaction.

Fulfill some of the fantasies you've dreamed about or admired in others. I've developed hobbies and interests of whitewater wilderness canoeing, writing, drawing, painting, singing in a chorale, teaching, and dancing, as well as identifying and leading walks to identify wildflowers, plants, trees, shrubs and birds. What about you?

Any hobby or interest opens up many new worlds of learning, discovery, shared interest with others, and a feeling of confidence and connection with that world of discovery. Building expertise strengthens self-esteem, the acquiring of more subtle levels of understanding and attainment, and leads to personal satisfaction. The option exists to teach others the creativity and satisfaction you are enjoying.

Creativity can be exercised with any process, too – whether cooking, playing a sport, exercise, leading or managing others, or playing board or card games. The mind, spirit and emotion want to be exercised each day. Creativity is essential. The spirit needs to be perked and lifted.

Maintain your unique self, discover new parts of yourself and listen for what you need to learn and experience. Don't initially go for expertise or goals. Go for enjoyment. Accept learning curves. It takes time and trial and error to "get good" at something. Instead, use play, patience, experimentation and personal growth as attitudes and actions to develop your interest, hobby or creative pursuit.

Creativity tips…

- Listen to your soul's desire to create – tune into what form that might take

- Admiring another's creativity might inspire you to try your unique version

- Avoid boredom by being creative

- Remember how satisfying it is to work on a creative project

- The initial few minutes or longer might be frustrating or "uncreative" – accept that – hang in there

- Focus on the joy of the moment as well as imagining a completed project

- Let the voice of creativity speak thru you or the creative project itself

- Practice makes "perfect"

- "Mistakes" help with the learning process – mistakes are necessary to develop – not time wasted

- Whether you let the spirit move you when to create, or whether you set time aside to create, spend the time you need to have fun exploring yourself

- Discover new parts of you

- Listen for the creative urge and act

- Watch out for negative comparisons to others – use others instead for inspiration

- Be your unique self and follow your calling

- Some people have lots of interests and some less – some go deeper with fewer things or have many interests with less depth – be you

- Get support along the way

- Go less for perfection and more for fun, exploration, play and discovery

- If discipline works for you, by all means use it

- The first few minutes might be a kick starter for something that works more easily in a while

- Relax and listen to your intuition and your creative juices might flow more easily

- Follow your own creative way – no one knows what is right for you but you

- "Try" less and play more

- Admire your creative work – learn from it – it has a life of its own

- Notice the negative voices (if any are present) and refocus back to what is supportive, helpful, useful, satisfying

- Enjoy yourself – in whatever ways work for you but if struggle, intensity or pushing motivates you, do whatever works

- Some people work in shorter or regular time lengths – others, hours and days on end – do what works for you

- Meanwhile, take care of yourself – eat, rest, work, and socialize if you need too

- Experiment

- Do a rough or several roughs before the final product

- Edit along the way – it can be fun

- Try many different ways before you find your most preferred rhythm

- Observe, think, sketch or imagine before you do a more final creation

- Don't get discouraged

- Create as much of a positive attitude as you can beforehand

- Create from your history, desire, emotion, thinking, imagination, memory or intuitive knowing

- Be inspired by others and possibly imitate in your own authentic way

- Use art to explore yourself and life, loss, pain, joy, anger or fear, integration or spiritual knowing

- Explore your child self, adult self, other worlds, the unknown, an imagined other self (I have elf and gnome characters I identify with)

- Allow your unconscious, subconscious and dream self to be open and allowing

- When truly being creative, time ceases

- Combine, integrate, combine or unite disparate parts of you

- Be powerful, vulnerable, flexible, boundaried or boundless during a creative enterprise

- Let your unconscious work on a project even when away from the project

- Work on several creative projects at a time

- Use your moods and feelings as inspiration – don't wait for a perfect state to create

- Ask for feedback along the way and be open to it, even if not delivered perfectly

- Thank people who offer you feedback, particularly in a useful way

- You are the author of your creativity so don't let others control or criticize you in a way that's destructive or limiting to you

- Never lose your unique way of doing it

- Let your intuition and need for creative satisfaction move you

- Listen to your dreams and longings from the past and fulfill them now

Nature

Nature is all around us. Animals, plants, trees, birds and bees are everywhere. Living things find whatever nooks and crannies or open spaces they can find. Go outside (or even indoors sometimes) and explore. Realize you are part of nature, too, rather than separate from it.

All living things belong here. Find the similarities in all living things – the striving to survive, to be unique, to adapt, to reproduce, and to live in community. Find out what is different in each species and appreciate it. Birth, growth, need for nurturance, competition with others, getting along with differences, flowering, loss, joy, rejection, growing older, and death are among things we all have in common.

Find ways to experience nature in its beauty – with walks in parks, nature preserves, camping, canoeing, hiking. Learn the names of plants, shrubs, lichens, flowers and birds, trees, insects. The more you learn about their lives, the more you will discover about them and yourself.

Explore nature in different seasons – and its many manifestations - rivers, oceans, lakes, rocks, mountains, and valleys. Learn what causes rain, snow, drought and floods. Study weather and cloud patterns and how they are created and how that relates to you. Pretend you are Thoreau (or just be yourself) and go for walks in nature every day.

Be your more natural self and use nature as a model. Look at cycles, growing seasons, and the earth as it moves and relationships with other beings and how they affect each other. Be touched by air, sun, wind, rain and snow and how that affects plants, birds, trees and animals. Be aware how they survive and thrive and what you have in common.

I've spent my entire life walking in nature, learning and growing, seeing patterns, visiting my bird and plant and tree friends, season after season, learning their cycles and seasons. Each year I look forward to seeing them, experiencing them, remembering them. It's a joy beyond words.

Nature tips...

- What happens in nature is symbolic of what happens in your inner and outer life

- Use nature analogies in your conversations

- Go for a walk in the woods or mountains, or on the shore of an ocean, lake or stream to refresh the soul

- Being in nature helps you get out of your personal problems and into the universal

- Nature helps you enter other worlds

- Nature reminds you to be more natural

- There are many groups and organizations that support nature walks – Appalachian Mountain Club, bird groups, plant groups, Audubon Society – most are free or low cost

- Pick an area in which you want to be more knowledgeable – wildflowers, trees, birds, insects, animals and start reading books and study guides, go online, go on organized walks, go by yourself or with a friend

- The list is endless of what you can explore – clouds, weather, rocks, geology, biology, stars, seasonal changes, caves, hibernation, bird migration, fish migration, seasonal changes, sun spots, etc.

- Watch nature shows on TV or watch nature DVDs

- Go on trips to national, state or local parks, organized or on your own – attend ranger or volunteer guided walks there

- Camp alone or in a group

- When feeling down, recall beautiful experiences in nature you've had or better yet, go outdoors for a jaunt

- Find new nature areas or parks to explore

- Find fellow travelers to explore with you

- Pick berries along your trip – june berries, mulberries, dewberries, blueberries, blackberries, huckleberries, strawberries

- Go to a talk or walk about edible plants

- Pick some edible plants to eat raw or cooked – make sure you have read some edible plant books or attended classes or gone on guided walks first

- While walking, smell the flowers, feel the air on your skin, notice the contours of the land, notice rocks, sky, moving things

- Be careful to the best of your ability not to step on any living things more than necessary

- Notice the ground as well as the trees and sky

- Bring water to drink, particularly on a hot day

- Have lunch on a special rock or meadow or near a stream, pond or lake

- Bring a bathing suit to swim if the water is clean and safe

- Bring a book to read – poetry, nature book, any book

- Exercise in nature – yoga, stretching, tai chi

- Climb a tree

- Look for lichens, moss, insects on trees, mushrooms

- Bring a camera to take pictures

- Ride your bike on a bike path or in the woods

- Sing or hum while walking

- Pick up leaves or nuts or weeds, fruits, flowers, seeds or pine cones to draw or add to your nature collection at home

- Bring a bird or plant book to identify what you see

- Go on bird or plant walks sponsored by local bird or plant groups or by Herb Pearce since I lead combined bird and plant walks!

- Many towns or cities have nature exploration bird, plant and animal identification groups such as in the Boston area - "Friends of Fresh Pond Reservation" that I below to for instance, "Friends of Mt Auburn Cemetery", "Friends of Alewife Brook", "Brookline Bird Club" and many of the walks are free or low cost

- Walk slow and see what's there – touch, smell, shapes, colors

- Walk quickly for exercise after you walk slowly the first time for viewing and learning

- Many towns have reservoirs around which to walk

Food

What we eat affects us. So many options exist of what to eat and the positive or negative benefits thereof. Our health, mental awareness and attitudes, emotions and decisions are affected by food choices, how much we eat and how we feel about eating. Family and cultural upbringing, how food is used as a substitute for other needs, and how we use food to nourish ourselves, affects our eating.

Traditional foods may or may not be healthy for us, even with generations of history behind the food. Cow's milk, for instance, propped up by romantic ideas related to dairy farms of our past and by the dairy industry, in my opinion, is unhealthy and indigestible for many people, yet continues to be advertised as healthy.

You have a right to experiment with what works for you. Try different foods, different settings in which to eat whether with others or alone, try different ethnic foods, restaurants, etc. Consider eating more slowly. Eating too much creates discomfort. Consider eating to 80 % of fullness as you probably will feel more full in 15 or 20 minutes.

Choose a food style that works for you. I am vegetarian and find that way of eating supports my health, well-being and moral consciousness. There are many options to bring food into lifestyle, diet and ways to support other parts of our life. Body image, eating control, pleasure, social sharing, and culture can play into food choices and individuality. There are thousands of eating options and ways to prepare food. Lifestyle choices include many ethnic choices, macrobiotic, raw foods, diet and food plans – the list is endless.

Of course drinking often goes with eating - so be open to drinking options too – water, fruit juices, rice, soy or almond milk, sodas, teas, coffee, yerba matte. Try new drinks. Cut juices or drinks with water if too strong. Alcohol can add to pleasure and social ease or can become an addiction if used too often to avoid life's pressures.

Food and drink can both be overused for relief, stress reduction or for stuffing down feelings. Like all substances or experiences, work with moderation. Instant pleasure may lead to pain, body discomfort, and unhealthiness. The body doesn't want to work overtime to process food it doesn't need or want.

We live in a culture that supports junk food, unhealthy foods and overeating. Work against the temptation for easy fixes, overfilling and indulgence. Food is meant to be pleasurable within a healthy limit.

Certain social settings encourage unhealthy eating or overeating. Be around environments, places and people that support health, balance and good food. Ultimately you are in charge of your body and you make the choices. Forgive anyone who supported unhealthy habits that you adapted. Meanwhile, whatever you do, enjoy eating and consider eating more slowly.

Food tips…

- You are what you eat

- Eat with pleasure

- Try a variety of foods and combinations

- Eat in a variety of settings and environments

- Have ambiance in mind when you eat

- Play music when you eat instead of watching TV

- Eat with beautiful views or in nature

- Eat outdoors, have picnics

- Eat one plate of food

- Go to potluck dinners, dinner groups

- Have lunch at restaurants – much cheaper than dinner and with smaller portions

- Eat only 2 meals a day and a snack for the 3rd

- Consider fasting with liquids for a day every so often

- Eating crackers, cookies, snack foods and artificial foods can be filling, yet addictive and not nutritious

- Have green smoothie drinks in a blender – avocado, nuts, fruits such as apples, mangoes and bananas mixed with kale, spinach or other greens. Try it with your favorite juice and rice or soymilk! Maybe add a clove of garlic!

- Eat some raw food

- Cut juices with water

- Eat soups, salads, fruits, and grains

- Eating well affects your health and well being in a positive way

- Eat food locally grown

- Eat organic foods, particularly from farms you know

- Eat a wide variety of colorful foods, especially green

- Explore edible wild plants – it's generally free – such as wild grapes, berries, Japanese knotweed, garlic mustard, dandelion greens, black locust flowers, parts of milkweed, cattails

- Drink teas from plant leaves – get a copy of Peterson's Edible Plants for guidance

- Cut down on excess sweets, carbohydrates, cookies, ice cream, pastries, etc. Good luck!

- Eat a limited quantity or calories a day

- Find substitutes for late night snacking – drink water, tea, eat fruit, call a friend, read instead – maybe eat a small amount of leftover healthy food

- Eating slowly might cause you to eat less

- Don't berate yourself – it only adds to the cycle of eating and berating

- Wait 30 seconds before you decide to eat excess food

- Don't eat just because it's in the refrigerator, or you are afraid to throw food away, or because it's a habit

- Many of us grew up in families that supported overeating – there's no need to repeat that – it can be a way to feel close to your family

- Watch out for people who want to nurture you by offering more food or overly rich or sugary foods – set limits for yourself or with them!

- If you are going to a special dinner or lunch, eat less during the day to prepare for that

- Commit to being healthy and having healthy food be part of that focus

- Hang around people who tend to eat healthier

- No one is going to starve to death in Africa because you didn't finish your plate – there are other reasons why that happens

- Buy fewer food snacks in plastic bags like potato chips, candy, cookies, vending machine food, etc.

- Reward yourself for eating well – without overeating!

- Picture yourself at the size and weight you want to be and focus on that throughout the day

- Weigh yourself or not, depending on what works for you

- Find other substitutes for food – affection, hobbies, social connection, books, movies, work, attending an event

- Be cautious during times of stress when it's easier to overeat

- Listen for and act when your inner voice says "enough," "time to stop"

- Enjoy the pleasure of eating, more than the "pleasure" of feeling full

- Some people tend to lose weight during a crisis – if you fit that, you might as well take advantage of any situation!

- Pay attention to how others use food in a supportive or non-supportive way

- Some people do well with small meals throughout the day

- Start fresh every day with weight or food goals

- Appreciate that food supports your body and life

- Say a prayer before you eat

- Pat yourself on the back with any small change

- Do the best you can and let go

Money

Money is as charged a topic as sex. Money is often tied to survival and security. In the past, many people bartered goods and services but today money is the main means of exchange. Money can also represent value, worth, a sense of power and influence, as well as access to experiences. Money itself is a medium of exchange, but it has grown to be the most important element of life for many people.

We have lost a balanced sense of self-esteem around money and its relative importance in life. Happiness can also be based on enjoyment, creativity, play, rest, relationships and communication, spirituality, learning - yet we often value those things less than money.

Money becomes the evaluation of success and the foundation of life instead of a balanced life. People worry, panic and have fear around money for survival needs and esteem. Money is overused as a symbol of worth and capability and it can take on life and death proportions.

Let go of overly comparing your money history and status with others. For instance, someone with a trust fund who doesn't have to work might not have developed a career that would be satisfying to him or her. Someone who is living on the edge financially may learn to use their creativity or live according to their social values instead of working in a job that has no meaning. They may live in the moment and trust the unknown.

Someone skilled in making money might be stuck in that mode and not invest in the learning required in relationship building. For some, money leads to greed and power and for others, generosity. Value what money teaches you and find the balance with money that works for you.

What does money mean to you? What do you sacrifice for it? Can you find satisfying and creative ways to make money? Do you work for money instead of having enjoyable work that supports you? Is your worth related to money? How does money relate to ethics? Where did you learn about the value of money? Some cultures value other things more, such as community, family support, free time, play, sharing, enjoyment, etc.

Consider money being an important part of life though not the foundation of life and your value. Integrate making money with creativity, enjoyment, and pleasure, supporting others, and doing what feels good to you. At the same time, make the money you want, enjoy what it provides, and have a positive relationship to money.

Priceless

Money tips...

- Making money can be creative and fun

- Don't evaluate yourself exclusively on how much money you make

- See money as a game to play – how can I obtain enough to live, survive, thrive, enjoy life

- Value what you offer so you feel comfortable charging what you are worth to others and yourself

- Make your money doing work that you love

- Prioritize what you want to do – play, build something, learn something, change the world, develop a skill and find a way that money can support that

- Do what you love and the money will follow

- Listen to your intuition or inner guidance about what to do to make money, spend money or invest money

- Focus on your purpose in life and let money follow from that

- People are willing to spend money on a service that supports them or solves a problem or adds value to their life

- Develop skills that people will pay money for

- Have several skills in case that one of them is no longer in demand

- Visualize having what you want – feel it, sense it, live as if you already have it – money will be attracted to that!

- See yourself as wealthy in whatever ways you are – whether financially or not

- Each day focus on how abundant you already are

- The universe supports you in whatever you do

- Understand the marketplace and how it works

- See money as exchange for services

- The supply of money can go up and down – don't let that be the guide to your self-esteem

- Trust that money will come in

- Prioritize what you want to spend money on

- Pay attention to spending your resources wisely

- Appreciate that you have money to spend

- Let go of comparing yourself to others and their money

- See money for what it can buy rather than a sign of your worth

- See money as a reflection of your personal values

- Use money rather than money using you

- Do exchanges with people that don't involve money - barter

- Find creative ways to attract money to you

- Do affirmations to attract more money into your life and that accomplish your money goals

- Feel that you are worth having the money that supports you

- Use money to make the world a better place

- Associate money with love, giving, balance, enjoyment and all good things

- Be around people who use money wisely, make money and have a positive relationship to money

History and Past

We all have a history and a personal story about our past. There's a tendency to string together that story to create meaning and continuity. It's great to create meaning, yet meaning changes with time, history is subjective and a negative or positive spin changes everything. We often picture a certain kind of life we want, which to some degree we can control. At the same time life happens the way it does and that needs to be accepted. Accept your unique history.

Prior generations, genealogy, family, race, culture, DNA and many factors beyond our control, influence what happens to us. Accept your historical backdrop. Be careful not to overly compare yourself to people who seem to have it easier or are more "successful." Everyone has their challenges and you might grow more or enjoy life more than the person who seemingly has it easier than you.

Don't spend an inordinate amount of time wishing your life were different. The moment of living or change is now. Often what is negative can turn out to be useful, growthful or even positive later on. It's all in the eye of the beholder.

Explore your past to understand it. Many insights can be gained. It's helpful to learn about yourself to not repeat prior mistakes. Learn while you grow!

Explore your genealogical background. It's fascinating to see your roots and how you may have been affected. The farther you go back, the more you realize how connected we are to everything. All of us can trace back our deepest ancestry to Africa, where human beings seem to have started!

Live in the present more than the past; yet value the past, the memories and learning. Keep letting go of anything that haunts you and live here rather than there. Don't relive traumatic or negative memories. Get support to let go and be here now.

History and the past tips...

- Write a autobiography of your life from a positive perspective on what you have learned

- Realize history is subjective – it depends on the premises or angles from which you are you viewing

- Be careful not to focus all your attention on the painful memories, traumas, etc. – otherwise your life might be victim oriented and unhappy

- The struggles and losses are part of the dance – make sure you pay attention to the triumphs too

- The struggles often give the strength to later move them to positives

- Your history can support you to be more empathic with others, add maturity, positive weathering and beauty to your years

- Heal your past

- Carry forward a more positive perspective than your parents and appreciate their struggles and how you gained from their sacrifices

- Help heal from your parents' past, but don't take on their karma

- Study history to see where people and society shine or go off course

- See the perspectives in which much of history is written – from the king's perspective, the peasants, rich people, merchant class, the middle class, the struggles, the successes, cultural or racial prejudices, blame, politics, nationalism, whitewashing, peoples struggles, spirituality, wars, peace, creativity

- Don't spend your life blaming your parents – understand them and their historical background, which can help explain why they did what they did

- It's fine to go through a period of anger in regard to your personal history and your parent's or other's neglect, control, abuse, or limitations – yet let it go at some point

- Forgive your parents after you have resolved most of the feelings toward them

- Be grateful that someone raised you

- Forgive your past – you are a product of your conditioning and need to see that most things are not personal

- Look at things from a social perspective – beyond the personal

- Understand your past but live in the present

- See what history has to teach you – what are your lessons?

- Enjoy the dramas and stories of your past without being overly attached to them

- How are you repeating your past?

- Keep healing any unresolved pain

- Focus on what's good about your past

- What do you want to do now different from your past?

- Find creative ways to understand and resolve your past

- Observe how others relate to their past – how are you to be similar or different in how you respond to your past?

- Write or journal about your past, write an autobiography, act out scenes from your past, talk about your past in a creative, useful way

- Recreate your past in new, creative and healing ways

- Share stories about your past with friends

Go Into Action

Things happen through action. Desire, clarity, commitment and action are the elements needed for completion. The completed dream is possible with support, not getting sidetracked by problems, and continued action.

So often people give up in the beginning before they actually start. The first sign of a problem stops the forward motion. All goals have problems and the solving of the problems is part of the creativity and fun and stamina building necessary for completion.

Get support from others too – possibly from people who have already done something you are dreaming about, people who can cheer you on, people who remind you of your dream, and people with creative ideas. People love to help you fulfill your dreams. Utilize their good will, which can support you to feel good about yourself. You can support them in their goals, too. Appreciate people and reward them in whatever ways feels good and real to you and them!

Make a "To do" list each day. Clarify and focus on your goals. Let go of some of the "how" of your goals. Trust that you and life will figure that out. Be open to the unfolding process and the learning and correcting and completion along the way.

The steps may change, and the process may be easier or harder than originally thought. It's best to first get the information you need in order to act, then act and keep learning. Don't put it off. Do something now and see what to do next. You'll feel better when you act rather than not.

Taking action is a way to release pent up energy from a too busy mind. The mind needs to follow through to feel complete. Don't act too hastily without inner focus and reflection – with no time to really process things. Find the balance between thought, desire, reflective time and action.

Action tips...

- Act, as a way to learn the next step

- Action can relieve the mind of worry and obsession

- You don't have to plan everything out before you act

- Follow your impulses, without being too impulsive

- Do some planning or have optional backup plans before action

- Action can be as simple as getting information, making a call, emailing, writing a note, or asking a question

- Take advantage of learning from others who have done similar actions to ones you plan to do – they may have the path laid out for you

- Get support to take action

- Remember times in your past in which you took action and great results happened

- Focus on the preferred outcome and don't overly worry how you will make it happen – just be committed to the outcome and the details will follow

- See obstacles as a way to learn what you need to learn – see them as opportunities

- Brainstorm ideas for action with friends

- Listen to your intuition on what to do

- Find people to mentor you who have done something similar to what you want to do

- Be willing to make mistakes, be humble, get feedback

- Be willing to "fail" to learn what you need to do to succeed

- Be patient, creative, forgiving and curious

- Read books, tapes, etc. about success and how people got to be where they are

- Act more than obsess

- See yourself as a person who acts rather than procrastinates

- You'll feel good when you act

- Set target goals and correct along the way

- Keep your esteem up whether you meet your goals or not

- Be open to a new goal showing up that may be different than the original goal

- Keep clarifying the tasks that need to be done

- Be open to the journey taking you where it takes you

- Be active, but also receptive to new ideas, listening, waiting

- Be around people who encourage you to act

- Reward yourself for actions taken, whether or not results follow – it will take you to your next step

- Reward yourself for results along the ways, as well as the final results

- Accept the learning curve

- Support others to act, set goals, give encouragement

Self-Esteem

We each are given a self, a body, mind and a unique personality in which to live and express. It's important to value the special gift we are given and treasure the opportunity to grow and create and develop. To utilize that gift, it's important to esteem the self that we have and to feed and nurture and feel good about it – enough to enjoy the ride and use the gift.

Esteem can be maintained despite circumstances or feelings – pain, hurt, and loss don't have to alter your esteem – even failure can occur without the loss of esteem. Of course it helps to accept your feelings and experiences and have a positive, hopeful attitude. Planning and action can certainly help with that process of esteem building and maintenance.

Build your esteem in all areas of life – work, career, money, relationships, friendships, health, play and fun, spirituality, personal growth, travel, security, etc. You probably will focus on some areas more than others. Instead of having your esteem be about what you accomplish, maintain your esteem in order to accomplish.

Work at building and repairing your self-image and feeling good about you. Make it about the effort as much as the outcome. Don't let anyone mar the way you feel about yourself and be around people who support you.

Esteem tips…

- Pay attention to what you like about you, your accomplishments and the qualities you have

- Trust people's positive comments about you and how you affect them

- Value yourself for the qualities you have as much as your accomplishments

- Feel good about your God given talents, as much as those you've developed

- You might not be as good at things that are new or a challenge to you – that's normal - don't let that affect you in a negative way

- Put some attention each day to maintain and build esteem by doing affirmations, saying or writing what you like about yourself and what you've done, writing about what you are looking forward to, what you are grateful for, etc.

- Focus more on what's good and notice the tendency to hyper focus on minor issues, the one or two flaws you have or the mistakes you made

- We all have flaws – it doesn't mean that something is wrong with us – we all need polishing

- Sometimes we call something a flaw when it's just a human growth curve or a tendency that needs working on

- Make a list of your good qualities

- Pay attention to the good qualities others say about you

- Treat yourself the same way you would treat a respected, loved friend

- Look in a mirror and be curious about the person you see

- Say loving things to the person in the mirror

- Do something each day to build your esteem

- Particularly when down or depressed or anxious, do esteem building and nurturing

- Value yourself for how you have given to others, how you've grown, what you've faced, what qualities and skills you have developed

- Appreciate that you've affected or contributed to the world in a positive way

- Ask for feedback from people about what's special about you

- Save emails, notes, letters, recordings that affirm you

- Focus on your successes more than your "failures"

- Esteem yourself for actions, qualities, attitudes, attempts and results

- Esteem others

- Make your life as close as possible to your dreams

- Do actions and activities that support your esteem

- If you love it, keep doing it

- Be less critical and more patient and loving to you

- You'll get good at anything you keep practicing

- Make sure your standards are yours, not others

- Love you for your adorability and vulnerability, just as you would an adorable or vulnerable child or some adorable thing they do

- Focus on the bright side and positive possibilities

- Make a list of what's special about you

Work

Most of us work or have to work to earn money. Hopefully we find ways to do this that are satisfying emotionally and rewarding personally, relationally, and financially. Our identity is often tied up with work - what we produce, how we make a difference and affect the world, how much money we make, and how others see us in our work.

Some of us work for others and some of us are entrepreneurs. Ultimately we all work for others – getting paid to produce some product or service that is beneficial to others, enough that others are willing to pay us for our service or work.

Work can get out of control though. The United States is particularly prone to a norm of workaholism – overworking as an addictive tendency. There's generally much approval and reward for this. Overwork and the extra hours entailed, often prevent a healthy balance of attention to relationships, enjoyment and personal development. Materialism and focus on money are often rated high on the list of importance in regard to survival and esteem - with other areas being less so. Relationships then, as well as other areas of life, suffer terribly due to not having the time to nurture them.

Focus on work being satisfying and rewarding. Get support from people who love their work, get paid well or adequately and who are often in touch with their life purpose and commitment.

Work ideally can support esteem, creativity, personal development, high ethics, great relationships and enjoyment. After my Work tips I'm offering a list of affirmations on How to Make a Living Doing What You Love.

Tips about Work…

- Do work that supports natural strengths, skills, and enjoyment

- Do something that betters the world

- Find ways to enjoy work

- Be grateful that work supports your life sustenance

- Create ways to transform work into an atmosphere of respect, creativity, helping others and the world

- Have your work environment be a place of beauty and warmth and whatever makes you and others feel good

- Support others to do work they love

- How can work support your creativity and good feelings about yourself?

- What is your life purpose? How does work relate to your life purpose?

- What are creative ways to do work, which can include hobbies and interests and still make money? For instance, I lead bird and plant walks for groups and families, as a side business. I would like to use my talent to draw portraits and paint nature scenes to make money, too.

- Listen to your calling

- Thank people whose work you like

- Be grateful to people you do business with

- Support others' businesses – eat at local restaurants or shops, go to workshops or trainings that support you

- Appreciate tellers, shop owners, sales people, and gas station attendants

- Help people feel good about their work

- Listen to people with work or work relationships problems and do your best to come up with creative problem solving

- Don't support workaholism as a norm, though it's fine to work as much as you want, particularly if you enjoy it

- Have less control, abuse, and blame at work - find ways to help rather than compete or put down

- Encourage people, including you, to enjoy work – to have fun and humor and support at work

- Clarify your work purpose and goals and see if that fits your personal life goals

- Be creative at work, take breaks, and learn from your work relationships

- Get support to do your work in more effective ways, to do work that you love

- Try on some new methods at work, to experiment, to learn from others

- Have your work environment be a visual place of beauty or sound or art or whatever supports you to do your work

- Take on tasks or jobs at work that are new or different – create new routines

- Appreciate that work supports you life and see work as pleasurable and rewarding

- Do part time work or have a variety of jobs you do

- Let go of ideas of what your work is supposed to look like

- Let go of pressure from family or friends about what you should do

How to Make a Living Doing What you Love and How to Enjoy Life: Whether you work for yourself or others

Affirmations:

- I deserve to do work that I love to do

- I deserve to be paid money for what I love to do – people would rather pay money to someone who loves what they do

- If I'm doing what I love, I'll be good at it

- It's my "duty" or karma to do work that I love

- Money can be an expression of love

- If you are happy in your work, you support others' happiness

- My destiny is to do work that I love

- Struggle and doing work you don't love, etc. is optional

- I can be/am secure financially and do work I love

- People need what I have to offer

- I serve others by doing work I love

- I love making a living doing work I love

- I clarify obstacles to "I love making a living doing work I love" and work through those obstacles

- It's ok to have fun, joy, satisfaction, peace, and harmony in my work – that is, it's ok to enjoy my life

- Work and play are both enjoyable

- I love spending time in life doing what I love

- I ease some of my fearful imagination and worst case thinking around work and money

- Security follows from doing my "destiny" – fulfilling myself with work I love

- I open to new ways of being and trusting and fulfillment

- I find ways to enjoy my work even if I don't love it

- I listen to my inner wisdom and not others' fears

- Doing what you love improves health, well-being and success

- Love what you do if you can't do what you love

- I define what's success for myself

- I am attracted to that which fulfills me

- Doing what I love improves relationships, helps others, and develops skills that I love

- I envision being skillful and satisfied in what I want to do

- I identify what I love and live out my destiny in a satisfied way

- I define life the way I want – not the way others want

- I am my own authority – I don't need others to authorize my existence

- I relax and breathe through my resistances and fears

- I am on the earth to play, learn, grow, enjoy, share with others and do what I love to do

- I love spending time doing what I want

- I have a good time in whatever I do

- I define myself rather than allowing others to define me

- I let go of controlling others and instead control myself in ways that still feel free

- Life is wonderful and making a living doing what I love supports that

- Doing work I love creates the challenges that are perfect for me

- I am free to be myself

BALANCE IN LIFE

It's easy to think about how life should be rather than how it is. We often balance between opposing parts of ourselves, dealing with complex realities, juggling limits and practicalities and how to have the various parts work together. It's a balance issue, not a right and wrong issue.

We balance time, complex moral issues, differing needs within ourselves and between others, and things that come up that we never imagined. We hope for easy answers and sometimes find fewer than we hoped for. Sometimes we give up part of our needs to make life work better in the long run. We realize we can't have everything we want, or at least without some sacrifice.

For instance, a strong desire to have children limits other personal wishes. A desire for stability or money may compromise the need for freer time. How you use your free time may be limited by financial choices. Wanting time alone competes for time that relationships require. Life is a constant act of balance, compromise and hopefully being grateful for such a wonderful dilemma – choosing between wanted options or the situations we find ourselves in and learn from.

Despite the difficulties, life will be more in balance with some relaxation, listening to one's self and others, accepting things as they are and attempting to change them through action. Focus on balance and go for as much as what works for you. Answers come with the focus on and desire for balance.

Balance tips...

- Include all the parts of you and prioritize what is more important now

- Sometimes we go for broke in one area and then balance that later

- We all have conflicting parts – let it be

- If you try to present an image that doesn't express the real you, you're always having to hide – most people will accept you for being real

- Be authentic, honest and complex and simple

- Chaos happens – find creative ways of dealing

- Balance conflicting forces

- If you are sad today, you may be happy tomorrow

- Sometimes you are imbalanced – so what!

- Things just are

- Focus on how to live a balanced life that fits for you

- Evaluate what you need now and worry about the future later

- Let go of how – just focus on getting there

- Balance attention between your emotional, mental, body and spiritual needs

- Other people often balance us out – hopefully you balance them too

- Self correct along the way

- It's the attempt to balance that helps you and others

- Trust that balance will occur if you focus on it

- If you are out of balance, what might you be avoiding?

- Are there really opposites or does your mind just need to see opposites?

- Life needs change and stability

- If you go too far in one direction, balance toward the other

- Be around balanced people or use them as models for a balanced life

- Shoot for moderation and the middle if that makes your life

- Let go of pictures of your former self – be you now

Herb's Coaching

Herb Pearce, M.Ed., is a therapist and personal coach, coaching people to enjoy life, value personality differences, and learn how to relate well to different personality types. He also teaches workshops on self-esteem, relationship building, communication skills, and spiritual development. He is an expert in the Enneagram personality typing system, teaching public workshops and organizational team building trainings nationwide.

Herb is the author of *The Complete Idiot's Guide to the Power of the Enneagram*, which you can purchase from the author as well as *Herb's Tips for Living*. You can receive Herb's weekly Tips for Living by sending an email to herb@herbpearce.com, or go to his website at www.herbpearce.com to sign up and to see his list of workshops in the Boston area. Call 781 648 3737 with any questions or to have a personal coaching session. Inquire how your group or organization can use Herb for personal coaching or workshops or training to improve your organization's communication and find effective ways to resolve personality conflicts and work together effectively.